After I'm Gone

A Play

Frank Vickery

A Samuel French Acting Edition

SAMUELFRENCH-LONDON.CO.UK
SAMUELFRENCH.COM

Copyright © 1978 by Frank Vickery
All Rights Reserved

AFTER I'M GONE is fully protected under the copyright laws of the British Commonwealth, including Canada, the United States of America, and all other countries of the Copyright Union. All rights, including professional and amateur stage productions, recitation, lecturing, public reading, motion picture, radio broadcasting, television and the rights of translation into foreign languages are strictly reserved.

ISBN 978-0-573-12003-9

www.samuelfrench-london.co.uk

www.samuelfrench.com

FOR AMATEUR PRODUCTION ENQUIRIES

UNITED KINGDOM AND WORLD
EXCLUDING NORTH AMERICA
plays@SamuelFrench-London.co.uk
020 7255 4302/01

Each title is subject to availability from Samuel French, depending upon country of performance.

CAUTION: Professional and amateur producers are hereby warned that *AFTER I'M GONE* is subject to a licensing fee. Publication of this play does not imply availability for performance. Both amateurs and professionals considering a production are strongly advised to apply to the appropriate agent before starting rehearsals, advertising, or booking a theatre. A licensing fee must be paid whether the title is presented for charity or gain and whether or not admission is charged.

The professional rights in this play are controlled by Samuel French Ltd, 52 Fitzroy Street, London, W1T 5JR.

No one shall make any changes in this title for the purpose of production. No part of this book may be reproduced, stored in a retrieval system, or transmitted in any form, by any means, now known or yet to be invented, including mechanical, electronic, photocopying, recording, videotaping, or otherwise, without the prior written permission of the publisher. No one shall upload this title, or part of this title, to any social media websites.

The right of Frank Vickery to be identified as author of this work has been asserted by him in accordance with Section 77 of the Copyright, Designs and Patents Act 1988

AFTER I'M GONE

First publicly performed on May 21st 1977 at the Sherman Theatre, Cardiff, and subsequently at the Eden Court Theatre, Inverness, with the following cast of characters:

CHARACTERS

Mam	Mavis Gibbs
Matti	Angela Griffiths
Edith	Glenys Lewis
Dad	Gareth Gibbs

The play directed by Brian Meadows
Setting by The Players Theatre

The action takes place in the living-room in a very ordinary house in a very ordinary part of Wales

SCENE 1 Afternoon
SCENE 2 Three weeks later
SCENE 3 Several weeks later

Time—the present

AFTER I'M GONE

Scene 1

A living-room. Afternoon

The room is in a very ordinary house in a very ordinary part of Wales. A door in the back wall leads to the hall, in which is a grandfather clock. There is also an entrance to the kitchen. The furniture consists of a settee with a small table behind it, a sideboard, a table with three chairs round it, an armchair and another chair. On the settee table are a few bottles of tablets and a cup of tea. On the sideboard some photographs are displayed

Mam is sitting on the settee, knitting. She drops a stitch and mutters to herself as she throws it at the bottom of the settee. She then picks up the cup of tea and sips it

Mam (*calling*) Matti? Matti? There's no sugar in my ... Matti? Matti? She can hear me, I know she can hear me, she just don't want to take no notice, that's all. (*Calling*) Matti? Matti? She knows I can't drink it without ... Matti? (*She starts to cough*) Now look what she's done. (*She coughs again*) She's started one of my coughing fits. (*She coughs*)

Matti enters from the kitchen

Matti What's the matter?

Mam coughs

Well, drink something, for goodness sake. (*Picking up the tea from the table*) Look, you haven't touched your tea.

Mam No, I couldn't. You didn't put any sugar.

Matti Of course I put sugar. You haven't stirred it, I expect.

Mam Well, there's no spoon, you didn't fetch a spoon.

Matti Yes, there's a spoon here, somewhere. (*She finds it on the table*) Look, here it is. (*She stirs the tea*) The sugar is still thick on the bottom.

Mam Well, I couldn't find a spoon. What did you expect—me to stir it with my finger?

Matti Knowing you, you didn't even look.

Mam Didn't you hear me calling?

Matti (*taking a duster from her cardigan pocket and beginning to dust the photographs on the sideboard*) 'Course I heard you calling. I think the whole street heard you calling. I was washing the dishes. I can't come at once, you know that. What was it you wanted, anyway?

Mam To tell you there was no sugar in my tea, gel.

Matti Is that all?

Mam (*after a slight pause*) Who's out there with you?

Matti (*stopping dusting*) No-one.

Mam I heard voices.

Matti (*just beginning to panic*) I was singing.

Mam Soprano and bass? I heard a man's voice out there as well as yours.

Matti (*hesitantly*), No, I don't think so.

Mam It's him, isn't it?

Matti Him?

Mam Yes, him. Selwyn Morgan. I told you, Matti, I don't want you courting no undertaker. I don't want him in this house, specially not after what he done to your father, God rest his soul.

Matti That was an accident.

Mam Accident? That was no accident, blind drunk—that's what he was. If I hadn't changed my mind and gone to have one last look at your father before they finally screwed him in, he would have been buried upside-down with a pillow under his feet, and I don't know what happened to his teeth neither, but they weren't in his head, I know that much. I hate to think where he might have put those.

Matti Aunt Olwen had them for a keepsake, don't you remember?

Mam No, I don't remember. And I meant what I said, mind, Matti, he is not to come in this house, and when I go—

Matti mimes Mam's last few words

—I want Arthur Davis to bury me; that's my wish. Nobody else, Arthur Davis.

Matti Oh, I don't know why you're making all this fuss. You know Selwyn's the best.

Scene 1

Mam He may be, but he's not burying me; I'll refuse to die first.
Matti Well, if you let me marry Selwyn he said he'd bury you for nothing.
Mam When I go, Matti, I want to be quite sure I'm dead. I wouldn't put it past Selwyn to bury me when I'm upstairs having my afternoon nap. And another thing if he thinks that, marry? Who said anything about marrying? He haven't asked you, have he? Well, have he? Have he?
Matti Yes.
Mam And what did you say?
Matti I told him I'd think it over.
Mam And have you?
Matti Yes.
Mam And what have that tiny little mind of yours decided to do?
Matti Well, I want to marry him, Mam.
Mam Against my wishes? You'd marry him without my consent?
Matti (*sitting next to Mam on the settee*) Oh, but Mam, the way I'm looking at it is this, I'm thirty-seven now, if I don't marry Selwyn no-one else might ask.
Mam Thirty-seven, and you think that's old, do you? Now look, Matti, your Aunty Dilys was fifty when she got married, and Uncle Edwin was fifty-five.
Matti Yes, and not one of them saw sixty.
Mam And I don't want no cheek from you, neither. I haven't taken it from you before and I'm not starting now, and we'll have no more talk about weddings, neither.
Matti But Mam, I want a home of my own.
Mam Oh you do, do you? This house isn't good enough for you now, is it.
Matti 'Course it is, but it's your house, not mine.
Mam Well, it's your house as well.
Matti Is it?
Mam Yes.
Matti (*rising and moving away*) Oh, so if I marry Selwyn he can come and live here an' all?
Mam No.
Matti But if it's my house as well as yours . . .
Mam I have changed my mind. It won't be your house until after I'm gone. No, forget I said that. I don't want to give him another reason for doing me in.

Matti Oh, but Mam, I don't want to wait until something happens to you. You might live till you're seventy.
Mam I am seventy.
Matti Look, I don't know why you're making all this fuss. If I marry Selwyn——
Mam If you marry Selwyn you don't set foot back in this house.
Matti And who's going to look after you, then?

Mam has not thought of this. She pauses, then speaks to Matti in a much softer tone, almost with understanding in her voice

Come and sit down, Matti. Come and sit by your mother.

Matti sits on the settee

Now look, Matti, it's not that I don't want to see you get married. No, I'd love to see you settle down with some nice young man before I finally close my eyes, but—well, you don't want to marry an old undertaker—now do you?
Matti Yes.
Mam Well you won't—not as long as I can stop you.
Matti But you can't stop me, can you?
Mam (*on the verge of tears*) You'd marry him and leave me here all alone with nobody to talk to or have a cup of tea with. I could die, and no-one would find me for days.
Matti But I'd call in and see you every day if you'd let me.
Mam Well I won't let you—and get up, you're sitting on my leg.
Matti (*rising and moving to the sideboard*) But Mam, I told him I'd give him my answer tonight.
Mam When did he propose?
Matti This morning.
Mam Took a lot of thinking over, that did, didn't it? Oh Matti, I never thought you'd turn out like this.
Matti Like what?
Mam Jump at the first man that showed interest. With a face like yours you can afford to pick and choose.
Matti But Mam, I haven't jumped at him—he's been asking me out nine years.
Mam Well, I always thought you'd marry somebody tidy, like a doctor or a dentist or somebody.
Matti I don't know why you're so against undertakers. We couldn't do without them, anyway.

Scene 1

Mam No, I know, but you don't marry them all the same, do you? Well, I know I couldn't. He'd be touching me, and I'd be wondering who he'd just laid out. Oh achafi.

There is a "yoo-hoo" from Edith, out in the kitchen

There's Edie. Go and tell her to come in.
Matti goes off to the kitchen

Mam arranges herself in a more comfortable position on the settee —she is now lying completely out on it

Matti (*in the kitchen*) Hello, Edie.
Edith (*off*) Hello, Matti.
Matti (*off*) She's in there.
Edith (*off*) I'll go straight in, then.

Edith enters, goes straight over to Mam, and shakes her by the shoulders

Oh, you are awake, are you? I thought you might be sleeping.
Mam (*in a very weak voice*) Come and sit down, fach, come and sit down.
Edith (*sitting on the armchair*) How are you feeling, then?
Mam Awful, fach, awful. I've only just come out of a coma.
Edith You're not looking too good, neither.
Mam (*a little frightened*) Why, what's the matter then?
Edith It's your eyes, they've sunk right back into your head.
Mam (*taking a small hand-mirror from the table*) Oh, they have an' all. (*Looking up towards the ceiling*) Why don't you hurry up and take me out of the way.
Edith Hey, come on now, any more talk like that and I'll send for the doctor.
Mam Well, perhaps he can have a look at Matti at the same time.
Edith Why then, what's the matter with Matti?
Mam It's her head. It's full of a load of old nonsense about getting married.
Edith (*rising and going to sit on the settee*) Selwyn's asked her, then?
Mam Yes, this morning. That girl's been more trouble to me than the worth of it.
Edith Pity she couldn't find a normal boy.

Mam She's beyond advice; she wants her own way and there's nothing going to stop her from getting it.
Edith She's always been a bit headstrong.
Mam Oh Edie, I don't want her to marry him, but I'm afraid to stop her in case she does something silly. You know what I mean, don't you? And the last thing I want is for her to bring trouble home.
Edith It's at times like this I'm glad I had seven boys.
Mam (*crying*) I don't know how she can do this to me, my own little girl.
Edith Don't cry, fach, it'll sort itself out.
Mam She don't seem to have no pride. She's forgotten what he done to her father; she wouldn't be doing this now if he were alive. He would have kept her under lock and key, but she don't listen to me, she never have. If I turned round and said, "Go on, marry him" she probably wouldn't even bother.

The play stops—the idea slowly dawns on them both to do exactly this. They look at each other

Edith Well, it's worth a try, don't you think?
Mam It might work.
Edith 'Course it'll work. You know what she's like—tell her to do one thing and she'll do something else.
Mam I don't know what to do.
Edith I know what I'd do.
Mam Chance it?
Edith Well, you can't do anything else, can you? And you've got nothing to lose.
Mam It's not what I might lose I'm worried about: it's what I might gain.
Edith Selwyn?
Mam Yes.
Edith Shouldn't happen to a dog.
Mam Every village have got one, but only my daughter wants to marry it.
Edith If only there was something we could do.
Mam It's not fair for a young girl to tie herself down to somebody like that.
Edith Yes, but if they love each other . . .
Mam I only want her to stop for a minute and think what she's

Scene 1

letting herself in for and . . . Love? Who said anything about love? Matti don't love him.

Edith Oh?

Mam No. She may think she do but she don't. And she won't—'cause I won't let her. Anyway, Mattie's too young to know what love is.

Edith Well, I don't know, I was twenty-eight when I fell in love.

Mam Yes, but there, you was always mature for your age, wasn't you? I remember in school, you were the first one in class to have hair under your arms.

Edith Come to think of it, you're right. All our family were the same.

Mattie enters from the kitchen

Matti Have you finished with that cup? I want to clear things away.

Mam (*pointing to the table*) Yes, there it is.

Matti picks up the cup

Just a minute, Matti, don't go. I want to have a word with you.

Matti Oh, all right.

Mam gives Edith a gentle kick. Edith looks at her and smiles. Mam kicks her again, harder this time. When Edith looks at Mam again Mam motions with her head for Edith to leave the room, Edith finally gets the message

Edith Oh, all right. (*She rises and takes the cup from Matti*) Give me that and I'll clear this away. You have a little chat to your mother.

Edith exits

Matti sheepishly sits in a chair

Mam No need to look like that, gel, I'm not going to bite your head off. I have changed my mind.

Matti What about?

Mam You and Selwyn.

Matti You mean I can marry him?

Mam If you want to throw yourself away, yes.

Matti Oh, but I wouldn't be throwing myself away, Mam.

Mam That's what you think, but there you are. I am not going to stand in your way. Just don't come crying to me when he wants you to do things you don't want to do.

Matti (*rising and sitting next to Mam*) What do you mean, Mam?

Mam You do understand about marriage, Matti? You do know what you'll be expected to do?

Matti Oh yes, and it'll be lovely—I know it will. Putting his tea, washing his shirts, mending his socks—oh, I'll love every minute of it, I know I will.

Mam (*after a pause*) That's not exactly what I meant, Matti. When I said "things you'll be expected to do" I didn't mean those sort of things. I meant other things.

Matti Other things?

Mam (*knowingly*) Yes.

Matti Like what, Mam?

Mam Well, like when he's tired and he wants to go to bed, and when you've both got there, he don't feel tired any more.

Matti Oh well, I hope he won't expect me to get back up again. You know me—when I'm there I'm there for the night.

Mam Look, Matti, I'm talking about the things married people do.

Matti Like what?

Mam You do know a bit about marriage, do you, Matti?

Matti Well, I know a little bit.

Mam Tell me, then.

Matti Oh no, I can't.

Mam Why not?

Matti 'Cause I can't. It's rude.

Mam Well, you can tell me. I'm your mother.

Matti is about to tell her, when she giggles

Oh no, I can't.

Mam (*shouting*) Oh, go on, go on.

Matti Well . . .

Mam Yes?

Matti Well, when they're in bed . . .

Mam Yes?

Matti When they're in bed and the light's out—(*she pauses*)—they kiss. (*She giggles again*)

Scene 1

Mam (*amazed*) Is that all you know about marriage, Matti? Don't you know how a woman has a baby?
Matti Well, I know where it comes from, but I don't know how it gets there.
Mam I don't think I'll bother to tell you that.
Matti Why not?
Mam 'Cause if I know Selwyn he don't know either, and the both of you will be better for not knowing.
Matti But I want to know, Mam. I want to know in case we decide to have a family.
Mam I don't think there's much hope of that. You're too old to catch now, gel. You've missed the boat.
Matti Do I have to catch a boat, then?
Mam Look, Matti, when you're married you'll be expected to do lots of peculiar things. Well, it's bad enough doing them with somebody who's handsome, but when it comes to doing them with Selwyn, well I couldn't—I know I couldn't . . . But there we are, it's not me that's got to, is it, and if you can bring yourself to respond, well, that's all right then.
Matti Respond? To what?
Mam (*shouting*) To his touch, gel, his touch—what the hell's the matter with you?
Matti Oh, he'll touch me then, will he?
Mam Yes, and if you're lucky he won't do nothing else.
Matti Oh, Mam, don't fret. I'm so happy.
Mam (*after a pause*) Matti, when your father passed away I had to go round to Selwyn's to sort out the business with his father, and he asked me in, and do you know, they didn't have a sugar-bowl on their table. They have a big black urn with "mam" and "dad" on it. It must have held about six pound of sugar. Well, if you can live with that, Matti, the best of luck to you.
Matti I don't care what they use for a sugar-bowl. The important thing is it's going to be our sugar-bowl.
Mam (*almost crying again*) Oh Matti, I wish you'd wait till after I'm gone. I don't like to see you like this.
Matti Mam, don't worry. I'm happier than I've been in a long time.
Mam (*frantically thinking of another obstacle*) I suppose you know all his faults, do you?
Matti What do you mean?

Mam Oh, it's important you know all his faults.
Matti I don't think he's got any.
Mam 'Course he's got faults—everybody's got faults.
Matti Selwyn hasn't.
Mam Oh yes, he has—he picks his nose. That's all he done in your father's funeral. And he wears his socks in bed.
Matti Only in the winter. And he won't anyway, when we're married, 'cause he'll have me to keep him warm.
Mam (*triumphantly*) And where are you going to live? Have you thought of that?
Matti Yes, we have. (*She rises and moves away*) Selwyn's father wants me to move in with them so I can look after him.
Mam And who's going to look after me, then?
Matti Or there again, we could all move in here with you.
Mam (*rising*) And I'll have to put up with Selwyn for the rest of my days.
Matti Well, it's either that or you move into Selwyn's house.
Mam (*shouting*) Me move in with Selwyn and his father?
Matti Or Selwyn and his father move in with us.
Mam You mean, when you get married Selwyn's father's going to live here an' all?
Matti Yes.
Mam Never.
Matti Well, something will have to be arranged. He's too old to live on his own and you're too ill to look after yourself. So it's either they'll have to come and live with us or we'll have to go live with them.
Mam (*crying*) Oh Matti, I never thought you'd do this to me. (*Shouting*) Edie! Come here quick before I do something I'll be... The death of me, that's what you'll be, my girl. The death of me. (*Shouting*) Edie! Edie! Edie...!

The Lights dim to a Black-out

Scene 2

The same. Afternoon, three weeks later

Mam is lying outstretched on the settee, presumably sleeping. Matti comes in from the kitchen, carrying a tray with dinner things. She puts the tray down on the table

Matti Do you want a cup of tea now, or do you want to wait for your dinner? (*No answer*) Mam? Are you awake?

Mam No, I'm fast asleep—can't you hear me snoring? No, I'll have it with my dinner. (*Sitting up*) What time is it?

Matti (*looking at her wristwatch*) It's just coming up to quarter to one.

Mam I thought you said that funeral was at twelve o'clock?

Matti Yes, it was. I don't know why he's late.

Mam Perhaps the men in the cemetery have made a mistake and they've buried Selwyn instead.

Matti Oh, he'll be here now just.

Mam What are we having for dinner, then?

Matti (*taking the fruit-bowl from the table and putting it on the sideboard*) Well, I've boiled you a lovely bit of haddock, you shall have it now with a nice knob of butter.

Dad enters from the garden carrying a folded newspaper

Dad I don't know whether you know it, Matti, but we're down to the last of the paper, in the toilet.

Matti I'll tell Selwyn to take more out this afternoon.

Dad starts to sit down, but just catches Matti saying the word "dinner"

Your dinner won't be long, Mam.

Mam All right, love.

Dad (*rising from his half-sitting position and walking over to Matti*) Dinner?

Matti Oh, I haven't done yours yet, Dad. (*Taking him to his chair*) You'll have to come and sit down again. I don't know what I'm going to give him, though.

Mam (*rising and going to the sideboard*) There's a tin of pilchards in the cupboard. We'll give him those.
Matti Would you like those, Dad?
Dad (*putting his hand behind his ear*) What's that?
Matti Pilchards.
Dad (*after a pause*) I think they're out the shed.
Matti Pardon?
Dad I said I think they're out the shed, gel.
Matti What are?
Dad Well, the pinchers, mun.
Matti (*raising her voice*) No, Dad, pilchards, pilchards—would you like them for dinner?
Dad No, I don't think so.

Mam takes a tin of pilchards from the sideboard

(*Pointing to Mam*) Do you?
Mam looks at Dad then at Matti, in complete bewilderment, then back at Dad again

Mam What?
Dad Think I'm getting thinner?
Mam (*handing the tin of pilchards to Matti*) Open them for him, Matti, and say nothing; that's the best.
Matti But what if he says he don't like them?
Mam Pretend you can't hear him.
Dad Selwyn's not back yet, then?
Matti (*loudly*) No, not yet.
Dad (*after a pause*) Is it raining then?
Mam (*sitting on the settee again*) What's he going on about now?

Matti moves to the table and prepares the dinner through the following

Matti Take no notice, he didn't quite catch what I said.
Mam Well, I don't know about being deaf, I think he's three-half-pence short of a shilling myself. It's not fair to you, Matti, he needs someone to look after him proper.
Matti I do my best.
Mam Oh, I'm not saying for a minute you don't. What I meant was that he needs someone to take an interest in him.

Mattie exits to the kitchen

Scene 2

Show him a bit of understanding. (*She rises and moves to Dad*) It's not easy though, is it?

Dad looks at her

Can't get through to you somehow, can we?

Dad says nothing

I say it's not easy when you've had no training.
Dad Is it raining, then?
Mam (*going back to the settee*) Oh Matti, he's hopeless.
Dad It was fine when I came in.

Matti enters with a plate of fish, etc., on a tray

Matti Do you want a bit of bread with this fish?

Mam takes a tablet from a bottle on the settee table

Mam (*as if she was still talking to Dad*) No, I can't eat bread, it lays heavy on my chest—what the hell am I shouting for? (*She swallows the tablet*)
Matti Do you want it by here or do you want it over there on your lap?
Mam No, I'll have it by here on my lap.
Matti Right. (*Handing Mam her tray*) Yours won't be long, Dad.
Dad What's that?
Matti (*going back to the table*) I said it won't be long.
Dad What won't?
Matti Your dinner. (*She butters bread*)
Dad Is it raining, then?
Mam Look, Matti, he's got plenty of money, why don't you try and persuade him to part with a bit and get him one of those hearing aids?
Matti Well, Selwyn's tried to coax him but it's like as if he don't understand.
Mam Don't want to understand, more like.
Matti (*stopping buttering for a moment*) Have he got money, then, Mam?
Mam Yes, plenty. He charged me a fortune to bury your father, and he owns half of High Street.
Matti But Selwyn haven't got any money.

Mam No, but he will have, won't he? (*Pointing to Dad*) When he goes to that big funeral parlour in the sky.
Matti Fish all right.
Mam Too many bones.
Matti Can't help the bones.
Dad I knew it wasn't raining because I wasn't wet.
Mam Did you hear that, Matti? He knew it wasn't raining because he wasn't wet.
Matti I know, it still hasn't clicked with him that we had the toilet moved indoors
Mam He needs someone who understands him.
Matti Selwyn does.
Mam Selwyn would. That's not the problem though, is it? The problem is to get him to understand you.
Matti It must be awful to be deaf.
Mam Yes. He can hear what he wants to, though, I expect. (*Raising her voice*) I say you can hear what you want to.

Dad does not look up from his paper

(*Shouting at full volume*) Oye!

Dad quickly looks up out front

I'm talking to you.

Dad casually looks over in Mam's direction

I say you can hear when you want to.
Dad Is it?
Mam Matti, I'm sure he does it on purpose.
Matti Do you want these pilchards hot or cold, Dad?

Dad does not answer

Dad?
Mam (*shouting at Dad*) Oye!

Dad looks at her

She's talking to you (*With exaggerated lip movements*) Matti wants you. Matti.

Dad smiles sweetly at Mam and returns to his paper

He don't lip-read very good neither.

Scene 2

Matti (*moving to Dad's side and putting her hand on his shoulder*) Dad, do you want them hot or cold?
Dad (*tapping Matti's hand*) Yes, I am a bit.
Mam Put them in a dish, Matti, and let him help himself.
Matti (*moving back to the table*) I don't know what's keeping Selwyn, he hasn't been this late before. (*She empties the pilchards into a dish*) Right-o, Dad, your dinner's ready. Come to the table.

Matti raises Dad and takes him to his seat at the table

I've done you a nice bit of bread and butter with the crusts off, just as you like it.
Dad (*as he sits*) It must be the weather.
Matti Well, I don't know whether to put Selwyn's dinner out now or wait till he comes in.
Mam Leave it and have yours. Nice bit of fish this, Matti, I'm enjoying this.
Matti (*standing just behind Dad*) I don't think he's going to say the same.
Mam No, look at him turning them round and round in the dish. If he don't hurry up and eat them they'll be bloody giddy.
Dad Matti?
Matti Yes, Dad?
Dad I don't like sardines, gel.
Matti They are not sardines, Dad, they are pilchards.
Dad They're too oily for me, mun.
Matti That's not oil, that's tomato sauce.
Mam Oh hell, he's colour-blind an' all now.
Dad I never have liked sardines.
Matti (*getting a little flustered*) Dad, those are not sardines, they are pilchards. (*Shouting*) Pilchards!
Dad Well, I told you, mun, they're out the shed.
Mam Oh give up, Matti, for God's sake, or he'll have you in hospital in a week.
Matti (*to Dad*) Look, do you want something else instead?
Dad What do I want to go to bed for?
Matti Oh, I wish Selwyn was here.
Dad Can I have a cup of tea?
Matti Yes, I'll pour it now.
Mam I'll do it, Matti, you sit down and have yours.

Mam goes and sits on one side of Dad, Matti on the other

Matti Thanks, Mam. (*Pause*) Well, have Edie been in to see you today?

Mam No, she'll be in this afternoon, I expect. Do you know, it took me three-quarters of an hour yesterday to explain to him who Edie was, and he still thinks she's my sister.

Matti He is a bit slow like that.

Mam Slow? He's stagnant. Do he take sugar?

Matti Oh, I can't remember.

Mam Hell—here goes. (*To Dad*) Sugar?

Dad looks at her

Dad Yesterday, I think.

Mam (*to Dad*) Right you are. (*To Matti*) Two.

Matti (*after a pause*) Hey he's not eating those pilchards.

Mam Can't blame him, really. I've had them in the cupboard ever since before the war.

Matti Oh Mam, you don't think they've gone off, do you?

Mam Gone off? In tins like that they'll last for ever.

Matti (*picking up Dad's dish*) They smell a bit strong to me.

Dad, not realizing that the dish has been taken away, continues to fork himself another mouthful, but looks astonished when he sees that the fork is empty. As Dad is doing this, Matti puts the dish back on the table. Dad looks at the table and sees the dish. He proceeds with his dinner, but as his fork is plunged for another helping, Mam picks up the dish and smells it. Again Dad is left without anything on his fork

Dad Bloody cat.

Mam puts the dish back on the table as Dad puts his fork. Fork and dish actually meet after some time. Dad looks at Mam in amazement

Mam Well, so would you if you'd been in a tin all those years.

Dad proceeds to put tomato sauce on his pilchards. He shakes the bottle vigorously

Did you hear that thunder last night?

Matti Awful, wasn't it? Selwyn couldn't sleep a wink.

Mam Oh aye.

Matti Couldn't find a comfortable position, he said.

Scene 2   17

Mam Not to worry, you've only been married three weeks, haven't you?
Matti (*looking at her wedding-ring*) Yes, Three weeks last Tuesday.

Dad empties the sauce in his dish, but the whole of the contents comes out in one shake. Dad looks at Mam sheepishly, but she has not noticed

Mam I can't believe it, somehow. My own little girl all grown up and married. I wish your father could see you now.
Dad (*putting his dish on the floor*) Puss, puss.
Matti What do you think he'd say, then?
Mam Oh, I don't know what he'd say, but you wouldn't be married, well, not to Selwyn anyway.

Dad drinks his tea from the saucer, then sits back and closes his eyes

Matti I don't know why you're so against Selwyn.
Mam I'm not against him, Matti. He's your husband, my son-in-law. It's not my fault I can't stand the sight of him.
Matti Well, he likes you, anyway.
Mam Likes me? Go on, he can't like me. I've never been nice to him long enough for him to like me. Hey, is he sleeping or have he passed on?
Matti Sleeping. He'll sleep anywhere. He was sleeping in the chapel of rest one day last week.
Mam There's a place to sleep. Anybody else there?
Matti Yes, Mrs Morgan milk.
Mam She went sudden, didn't she?
Matti In the butcher's, she was.
Mam Younger than me, too.
Matti Never.
Mam Yes. Well, that's life, isn't it. You don't know where you are—here today, gone tomorrow

Mam looks at Dad, who is still sleeping, but his top set of teeth is now hanging from his mouth

Matti (*looking at Dad*) Dad?
Mam Are you sure he's all right? (*Rising and going to the settee*) Achafi.
Matti (*shaking Dad by the shoulder*) Dad, you haven't drunk your tea.

Dad (*waking up*) Who's there? Where's Selwyn, then?
Matti He hasn't come back yet. (*To Mam*) Hey, I'm getting a bit worried now.
Mam Oh, don't fret, he'll be here in a minute.
Matti Well, I'll just go out the front to see if he's coming up the road.

Matti goes out

Mam coughs. Pause. Dad coughs. Pause. Mam coughs. Pause. Dad coughs. Mam coughs

The Lights fade to a Black-out on a chorus of coughing

SCENE 3

The same. Several weeks later

The furniture has been changed around to some extent (see plan of set on page 27)

Matti is hoovering the room. After a few seconds there is a "yoo-hoo" from outside. Matti switches off the cleaner and listens. Hearing nothing, she switches on again. There is another call from outside, but Matti does not hear. Edith comes into the hallway and calls into the room

Edith Anybody in?

Matti continues to clean. Edith walks over to her

Anybody? (*She touches Matti on the arm*)
Matti (*jumping*) Oh, you frightened me, then. Come in, Edie, sit down.
Edith Busy, are you?
Matti Just hoovering up a bit, that's all.
Edith I popped in to see you and have a chat, but if you're busy...
Matti No, no, sit down, sit down.

Edith sits

I'll put the kettle on now, just let me finish by here first. (*She*

cleans towards the sideboard) It's nice to see you, Edie. You should call more often. I don't get much company these days.
Edith I bet you find it strange, do you?
Matti Oh yes, but it's surprising how soon you get used to it. Keep busy, that's the secret, I think. Never got time to think about it then.
Edith I can't believe they've gone, somehow.
Matti Yes, well, that's how it goes, I suppose.
Edith Funny for them both to go like that, though, isn't it?
Matti I still haven't quite got over it.
Edith Well, it was a shock, gel. How long has it been now, two months?
Matti No, it'll be nine weeks now, come Friday. (*She switches off the hoover and puts it beside the sideboard*)
Edith Don't time fly?
Matti Frightening, isn't it.
Edith Only seems like last week it happened. How's Selwyn taking it?
Matti Oh, in his stride, I think. Now then, the kettle.

Mattie exits to the kitchen

(*off*) He don't talk about it much. He haven't got time to think about it though, really. He's been too busy.
Edith How's business?
Matti (*off*) Oh, marvellous. They're dropping off like flies.
Edith It's that last lot of cold weather that's doing it, I'm sure.

Matti enters carrying a tray with tea things

Matti Been bitter, haven't it.
Edith A killer.

Matti sits at the table and prepares the tea

Eh, I heard in the bakehouse this morning that Mrs Jones is very low.
Matti Mrs Jones?
Edith Yes, you know, gel. The one who lives next door but one to the betting shop.
Matti Betting shop? Can't place her.
Edith Yes, you know her. Her eldest girl married that boy who had a bit of trouble that time.
Matti Trouble?

Edith Yes, you know. (*She mouths a load of nonsense which only Matti understands*)

Matti Oh, that Mrs Jones.
Edith Got her now?
Matti Yes, I know the one. She shaves, don't she?
Edith That's her.
Matti Very low, is she?
Edith Not much coming from her, I heard.
Matti I'll tell Selwyn when he comes down.
Edith Upstairs, is he?
Matti Yes, he's gone to bed for an hour.
Edith Nice, too. I used to like an hour in the afternoon myself.
Matti Don't you any more, then?
Edith No, I haven't bothered since Dai died.
Matti Two sugars for you, is it?
Edith And not a lot of milk. I can't stand milky tea.
Matti Well, you're looking well, Edie. How are you keeping?
Edith Oh, not so bad. I still get that same trouble, mind you, but it comes and goes so I can cope with it.
Matti That's not too much milk in it?
Edith No, no, that's lovely. (*Pause*) You've put on a bit of weight, Matti; married life suits you.
Matti It's all the tea I'm drinking. That's all I've been doing lately. I went through a pound and a half of tea last week, and there's only the two of us now.
Edith Sure you're not going in for a little tea-bag? (*She laughs*)
Mam (*off, calling*) Matti? Matti? Put the kettle on, I'm as dry as a cork.

Mam enters

Hello, Edie, it's nice to see you. (*She sits in the armchair*) I haven't seen you for ages.
Edith No, and I haven't seen you neither. (*Looking round the room*) Well, where is he, then? Where's the man of the moment, your husband?
Mam He's coming up the hill. He couldn't keep up with me; he haven't got the chest I've got.
Edith He'd look a bit funny if he did, eh?

They laugh

Scene 3

Mam Oh Edie, you're awful.
Matti Why didn't you write you were coming, Mam?
Mam Thought I'd surprise you.
Matti But I haven't aired the bed.
Mam If that's an excuse not to have us, Matti, just say the word and we'll catch the next train home.
Matti (*to Edith*) She hasn't changed a bit, have she? Still as touchy as she used to be.
Edith Do you like living away?
Mam Oh yes. Never thought I would, mind. Never thought I'd leave this place. Funny how you change your mind, i'n it? You should come up and visit us for a few days, Edie.
Edith Yes, I'd like that.
Mam (*to Matti*) Where's Selwyn, then?
Matti In bed.
Mam Bad, is he?
Matti No, tired, that's all
Mam Well, you'd better tell him we're here.
Matti Yes, I will in a minute.
Mam How are you keeping then, Edie, all right?
Edith Yes, not too bad, see.

Matti goes to the kitchen to fetch two more cups

Hey, Williams the whiperene's dead.
Mam Never! He's never dead?
Edith Well, they buried him, anyway.

They both laugh

Mam Oh Edie, you're a hell of a girl. How do you get on with your new neighbours?
Edith Which ones?
Mam Well, the ones in number seventeen—there's nobody else, is there?
Edith Yes, Mr and Mrs Thomas from next door sold up and moved to Cardiff three weeks ago.
Mam Cardiff? I always said they were snobs.
Edith Horrible they are, the people that moved in instead. Always borrowing, borrowing all the time. But the people in number seventeen are nice enough, though. Haven't been married long. He's got a good job with the Co-op, and her father's a manager of a colliery somewhere.

Mam No children, is there?

Matti comes in with two cups and saucers

Edith No, but they've lost two, one after the other. She can't carry them long for some reason. She's going in now to find out what's the matter.

Mam
Edith } Internal. (*Speaking together*)

Mam Oh, you know them pretty well, then?

Edith Pretty well? No, once she's spoken to me since they moved in.

Dad enters the room, gasping for breath. He is carrying a bunch of flowers

Dad I'm just about worn out. (*He sees Matti, goes to her and gives her the flowers*) Hello, Matti, fach. (*He sees Edith*) Hello, Olwen.

Mam She's Edie. I've told you before, she's Edie.

Edith (*to Dad*) I'm Edie.

Dad Easy? Achafi. (*He sits*) Selwyn's not here yet, then, is he?

Matti No, he's in bed.

Dad Where?

Mam (*raising her voice*) In bed.

Dad Where?

Mam (*pointing to the ceiling*) Bed.

Dad (*shocked*) Dead?

Mam (*shouting*) Bed! Bed! What the hell's the matter with you?

Dad Oh, shall I have a cup of tea?

Matti (*giving Dad a cup*) How are you, then, Dad?

Dad Hello, fach.

Matti How are you?

Dad Nice to see you.

Matti How are you?

Dad Selwyn's not down yet, then?

Matti No, not yet. You're all right, then, Dad?

Dad How are you, fach?

Matti Oh, I'm lovely. How are you?

Dad Yes, thank you.

Edith (*to Mam*) Well, I'm off now, then. (*She rises*)

Mam Oh, don't go yet, gel, I've only just come.

Scene 3

Edith No, I'll have to go. I've got a nice bit of bacon boiling. I'll call in later on, though, if you like.
Mam Yes, all right. Don't forget.

Edith starts to go, then turns to Mam

Edith Had I better say so-long to him?
Mam Well, you can try.
Edith (*going to Dad*) I'm off now, then.

Dad will not have anything to do with her

I'll see you later, then.

Dad makes a face and turns away

He's awful deaf, i'n he?

Edith goes

Mam So you're all right, then, Matti? Put on a bit of weight, though, haven't you?
Matti Edith said that as well.
Mam Sure you're all right?
Matti Never felt better.
Mam I expect you're wondering why we've come?
Matti No.
Mam Don't tell lies, Matti. It's written all over your face.
Matti You'll tell me when you're ready to, I expect.
Mam That's what gets me with you, Matti, you're not nosey at all.
Matti (*after a pause*) You're looking well, Mam.
Mam I feel well.
Matti Well, you look well.
Mam (*shouting*) Well, I feel well.
Matti (*after a pause*) Did you have a nice journey?
Mam No. Don't like trains—never have.
Matti Well, why didn't you come by bus, then?
Mam 'Cause he wanted to come by train. You don't know what he's like, Matti. When he puts something into his head there's no stopping him. Train he wanted, and train it had to be.

Dad looks at her

Still, I can't complain, he's ... (*To Dad*) go upstairs and tell Selwyn.

Dad (*handing his cup to Matti*) Go upstairs and tell Selwyn?
Mam Yes.
Dad Go upstairs and tell Selwyn.
Mam Now.
Dad (*rising and going to the hall*) Go upstairs and tell Selwyn now.

He exits to the hall then comes back

Tell him what?
Mam (*shouting*) Oh, go on, go on.

Dad goes

Matti Don't shout.
Mam No, I shouldn't shout at him, really. He's good to me, Matti. He's made a new woman out of me. I feel better than I have for years.
Matti So you're happy, then?
Mam Happy? Well, I wouldn't say I'm happy. I mean, I've lost my independence, but I've gained a bank account.
Matti But you haven't got any money, Mam.
Mam No, I know but he have, and we've got a joint account now. He don't quite understand it, mind. He thinks I'm having meat on tick.
Matti (*laughing*) Oh, Mam! So you are happy?
Mam I tell you, Matti, since I married him the world is my cockle.
Matti Oyster.
Mam What?
Matti Nothing.
Mam That's right. (*Pause*) Oh, it's no good, Matti, I can't keep it in any longer. I've got a surprise for you.
Matti Oh Ma, you've not been buying presents, have you?
Mam No, better than that. (*She opens her handbag and takes out four tickets*) Here they are.
Matti What are they?
Mam Tickets.
Matti Tickets?
Mam Yes, for the *Queen Elizabeth*. We are going on a cruise.
Matti Oh Mam, you and the Queen going on a cruise.
Mam No, mun, me and Dad and you and Selwyn. A cruise round the world. Can you imagine it, Matti? Around the world. The furthest I've ever been is Treorchy.

Scene 3

Matti (*taken up by Mam's excitement*) Around the world in eighty days.
Mam Only, this isn't going to take eighty days, Matti. It's going to take fourteen weeks. Fourteen weeks.
Matti (*elated*) I've seen the film. I've always wanted to go up in one of them things.
Mam The *Queen Elizabeth* is a boat, mun, not a bloody balloon.
Matti Am I going to catch a boat, then?
Mam Yes.
Matti (*putting her hands on her stomach*) Oh.
Mam We do fly, though. The man in the travelling shop said it was—um—just a minute, I've written it down somewhere. (*She brings out a piece of paper from her bag and shows it to Matti*)
Matti (*reading it*) Supersonic.
Mam Yes, that's right, supercronic.
Matti I'm going to catch a boat.
Mam And we are paying for everything.
Matti (*looking at her stomach*) I'm going to catch a boat.
Mam You and Selwyn are not to put your hands in your pockets for nothing, Dad said.
Matti What did he say?
Mam Oh, I'll never forget it, Matti. It's engrained in my heart. He looked up at me and he said, "What good is money in the bank," he said, "let's spend it while we're here." And I said, "Dad," I said, "that's fine by me." And just so that we'll have a bit of peace on the cruise, I've bought him a present. (*She takes a hearing aid out of her bag*) It's the latest, most up-to-date electronically tested, computerized, compastorized, earing aid. (*She empties her bag on the table*) And enough bloody batteries to last the whole trip.

Dad comes rushing in

Dad Here's Selwyn. Here he is coming.
Mam (*shouting*) Selwyn? Selwyn? Selwyn?

They all turn to see Selwyn come into the room, as the Lights fade quickly to a Black-out, and—

the CURTAIN *falls*

FURNITURE AND PROPERTY LIST

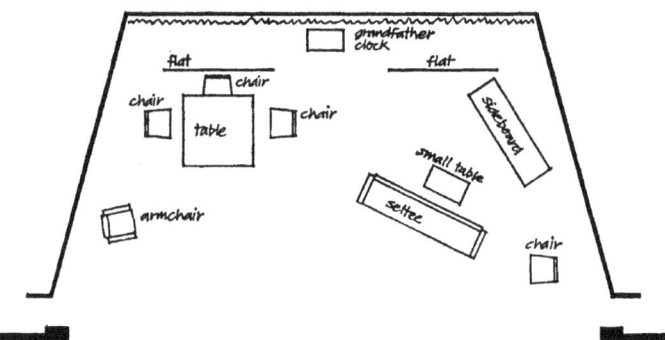

On stage: Settee. *On it:* cushions, knitting
Armchair
4 small chairs
Settee table. *On it:* cup of tea, teaspoon (separate), bottles of tablets, small hand-mirror
Grandfather clock
Table. *On it:* cloth, fruit-bowl
Sideboard. *On top:* family photographs. *In cupboard:* tin of pilchards with opener

Off stage: Duster (**Matti**)
Tray with various dishes, cutlery, bread, butter, bread-knife, teapot, milk-jug, sugar-bowl, tomato sauce (**Matti**)
Newspaper (**Dad**)
Tray with plate of fish, knife, fork (**Matti**)
Hoover (**Matti**)
Tray with 2 cups, 2 saucers, teapot, milk jug, sugar-bowl (**Matti**)
2 cups, 2 saucers, 2 teaspoons (**Matti**)
Bunch of flowers (**Dad**)

After I'm Gone

Personal: **Matti:** wristwatch, wedding-ring (Scene 2)
Dad: false teeth
Mam: handbag with 4 travel tickets, hearing-aid and several batteries, piece of paper (Scene 3)

After SCENE 1:

Strike: Knitting

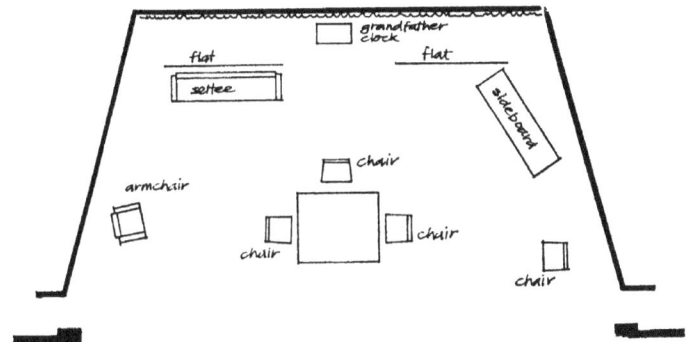

After SCENE 2:

Strike: Settee table
All dishes and cutlery
Tray of fish

Set: Furniture in new positions (*see plan*)

LIGHTING PLOT

Property fittings required: nil
Interior. A living-room

To open: General effect of afternoon light

Cue 1	**Mam:** "Edie! Edie! Edie!" *Fade to Black-out, bring up to previous lighting for Scene 2*	(Page 10)
Cue 2	**Mam** and **Dad** cough *Fade to Black-out, bring up to previous lighting for Scene 3*	(Page 18)
Cue 3	**Mam:** "Selwyn? Selwyn? Selwyn?" *Quick fade to Black-out*	(Page 25)

Printed by
THE KINGFISHER PRESS, LONDON NW10 6UG

www.ingramcontent.com/pod-product-compliance
Lightning Source LLC
Chambersburg PA
CBHW070455050426
42450CB00012B/3281